a b c d e f g h i
A B C D E F G H I

j k l m n o p q r
J K L M N O P Q R

s t u v w x y z
S T U V W X Y Z

A a

ant

ants

This is an ant.

Ants have six legs.
They walk.

B b

bird

birds

This is a bird.

Birds have two legs and two wings.
They fly.

3

C c

chair

chairs

This is a chair.

Chairs have a back and four legs.

But they don't walk!

D d

dog

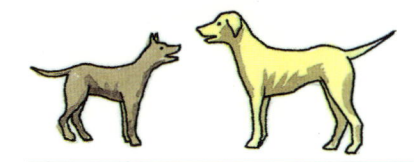

dogs

This is a dog.

Dogs have four legs and a tail.
They run and bark.
They are animals.

E e

egg

eggs

This is an egg.

Eggs don't have legs!

F f

fish

fish

This is a fish.

Fish have a tail, but they don't have legs. They swim.

G g

goat

goats

This is a goat.

Goats have four legs and a tail.
They are animals, like dogs.

They eat anything.

8

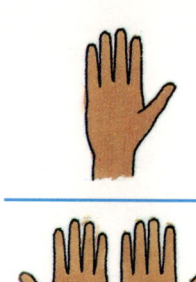

H h

hand

hands

This is a hand.

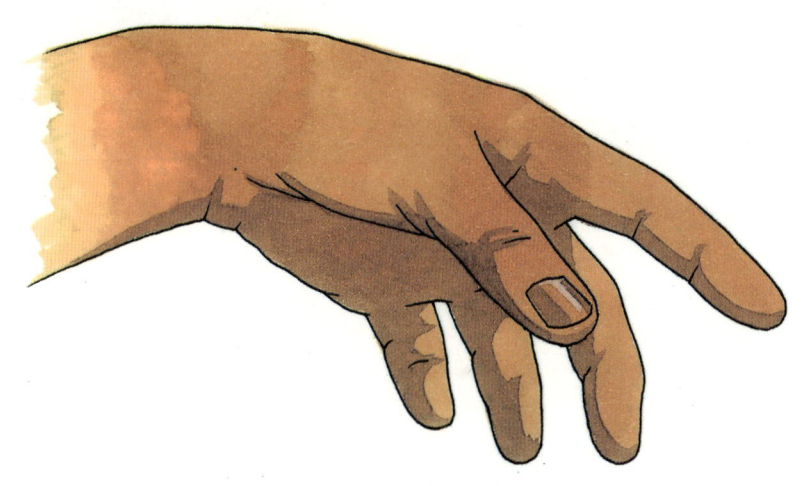

We hold things with our hands.

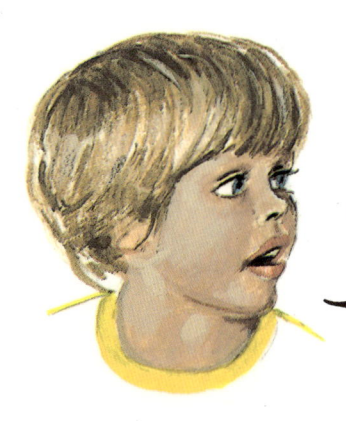

Animals don't have hands. They have paws.

I i

insect

insects

An ant isn't an animal.
It's an insect.

These are insects, too.

Insects have six legs.
Most insects have wings, too.

J j

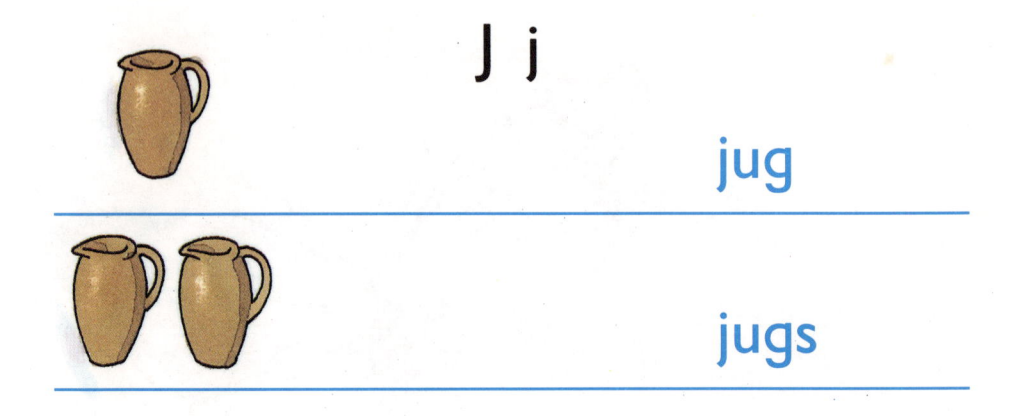

jug

jugs

This is a jug.

Jugs have handles.

This is a jar.

Do jars have handles?

K k

kitten

kittens

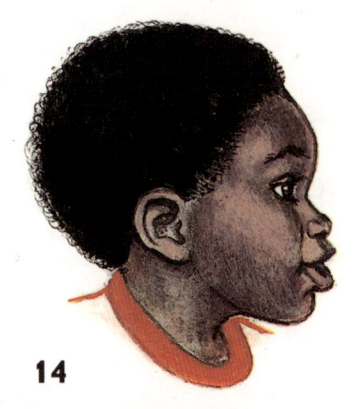

This is a kitten.

Kittens don't have tails. Is that true?

14

L l

lizard

lizards

This is a lizard.

And this is a snake.

Lizards have legs, but snakes don't.

M m

man

men

This is a man.
He has a hat on his head.

Men talk a lot.

N n

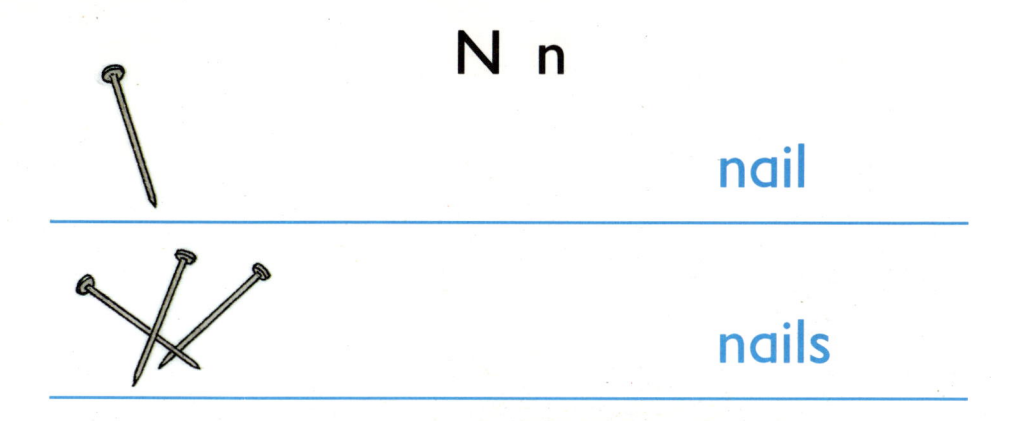

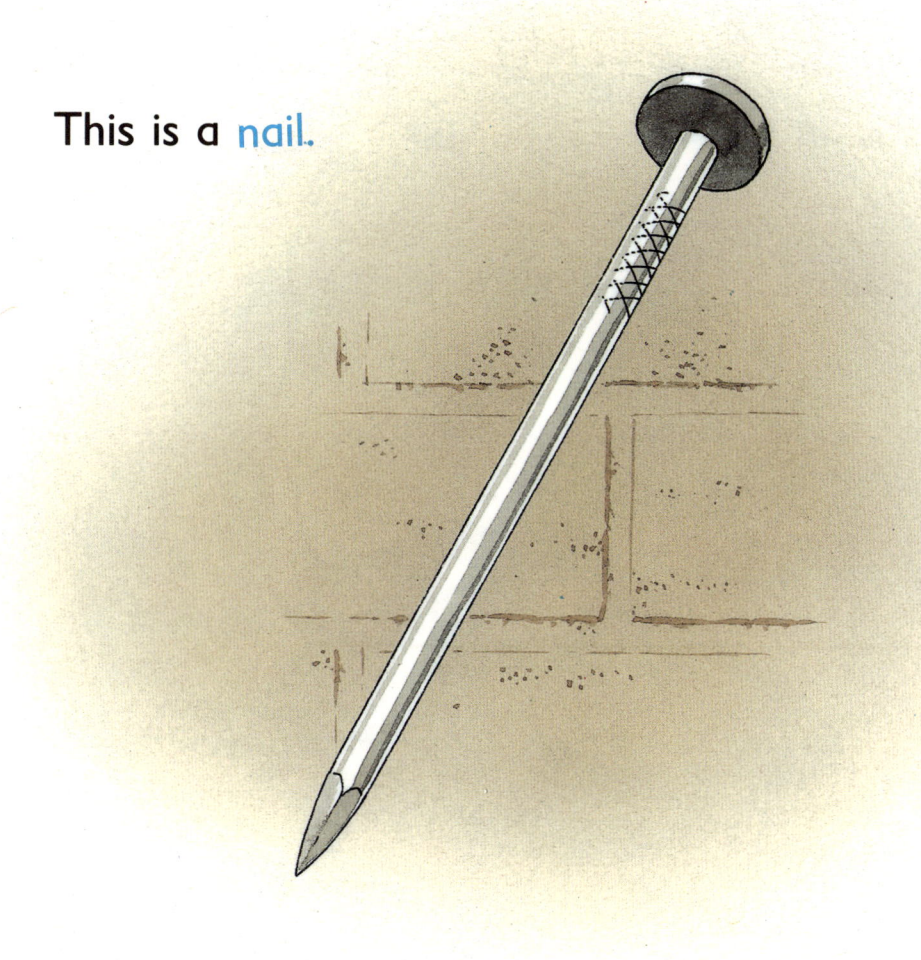

nail

nails

This is a nail.

Nails have a head at one end.
The other end is a point.

O o

ostrich

ostriches

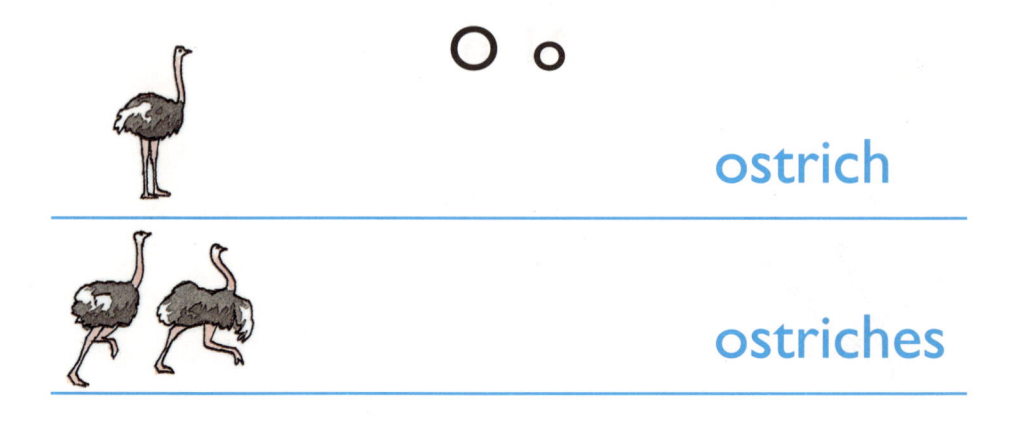

This is an ostrich.

Ostriches have wings, but they don't fly.
They sit on their eggs.

P p

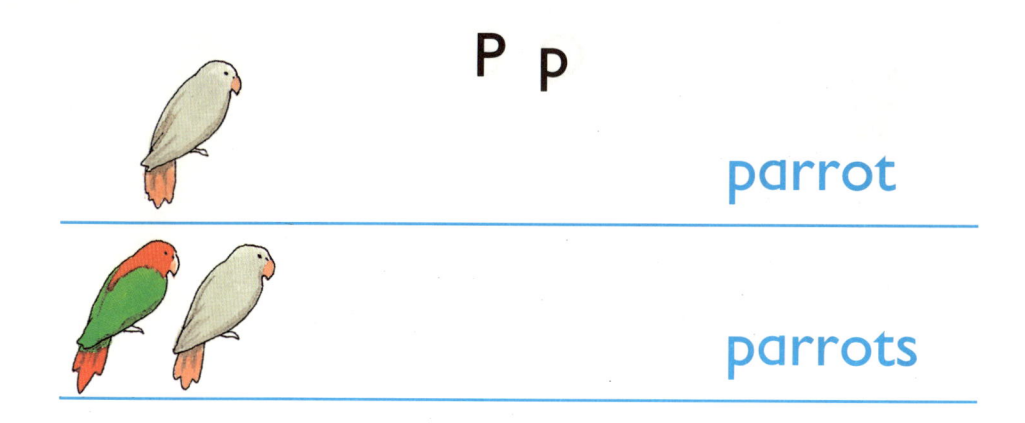

parrot

parrots

This is a parrot.

It can fly and it can talk.

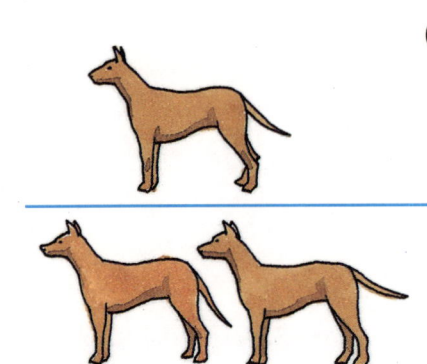

Q q

quadruped

quadrupeds

This is a quadruped.

This is also a quadruped.
Quadrupeds walk on four legs.

Are you a quadruped?

R r

rat

rats

This is a rat.

Rats aren't animals. They're insects. Is that true?

S s

stool

stools

This is a stool.

Stools have three legs, or four.

But they don't have a back.

T t

table

tables

This is a table.

Tables have four legs and a top.

23

U u

umbrella

umbrellas

This is an umbrella.

Umbrellas have handles. Is that true?

V v

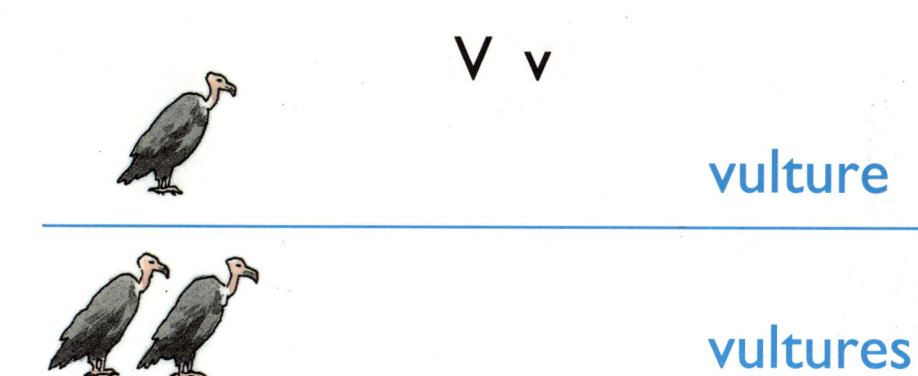

vulture

vultures

This is a vulture.

Vultures fly high in the sky.

25

W w

woman

women

This is a woman.
She has bangles on her arms and legs.

Has she got a jug on her head?

26

Women talk a lot. Is that true?

X x

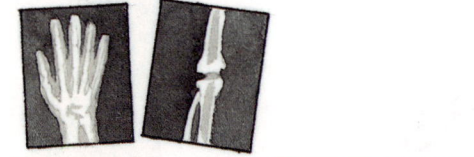

x-ray

x-rays

This is an x-ray.

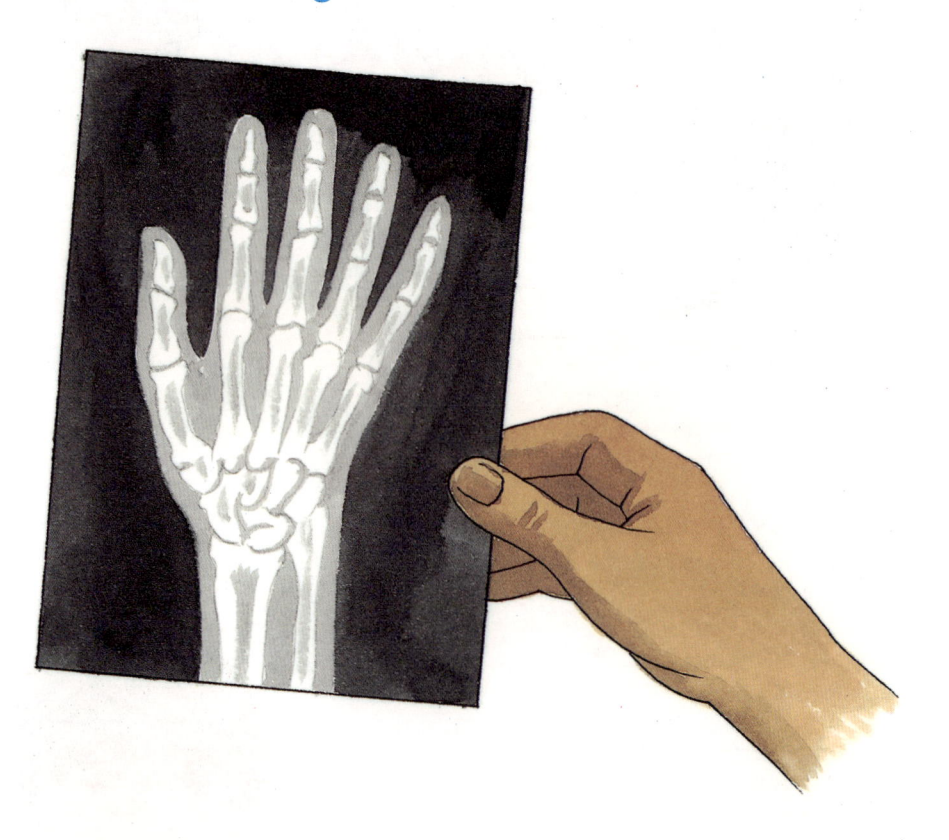

X-rays can see the bones in your hand.

Y y

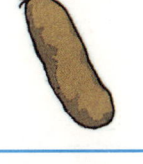

yam

yams

This is a yam.

Yams don't have legs, but they can climb!

Z z

zoo

zoos

This is a zoo.

In some countries children can only see these animals in zoos.

HOP STEP JUMP

HOP

In My Father's Village Michael Palmer
Striped Paint Rosina Umelo
The Slow Chameleon and **Shammy's Bride** David Cobb
The Walking Talking Flying ABC David Cobb

STEP

Choose Me! Lynn Kramer
Nondo the Cow Diane Rasteiro
Sika in the Snow David Cobb

JUMP

Chichi and the Termites Wendy Ijioma
The Boy who ate a Hyena James G D Ngumy
Tickets for the Zed Band Lynn Kramer

© Copyright text David Cobb 1992
© Copyright illustrations The Macmillan Press Ltd 1992

All rights reserved. No reproduction, copy or transmission of this publication may be made without written permission.

No paragraph of this publication may be reproduced, copied or transmitted save with written permission or in accordance with the provisions of the Copyright, Designs and Patents Act 1988, or under the terms of any licence permitting limited copying issued by the Copyright Licensing Agency, 90 Tottenham Court Road, London W1P 9HE.

Any person who does any unauthorised act in relation to this publication may be liable to criminal prosecution and civil claims for damages.

First published 1992
Reprinted 1994

Published by THE MACMILLAN PRESS LTD
London and Basingstoke
Associated companies and representatives in Accra, Auckland, Delhi, Dublin, Gaborone, Hamburg, Harare, Hong Kong, Kuala Lumpur, Lagos, Manzini, Melbourne, Mexico City, Nairobi, New York, Singapore, Tokyo

ISBN 0-333-56864-8

Printed in Hong Kong

A catalogue record for this book is available from the British Library.

Illustrations by DAVID WOODROFFE and JOAN GAMMANS